Google Classroom

Best Google Classroom Guide for the Teacher

© **Copyright 2017 by James Bird - All rights reserved.**

The following eBook is reproduced below with the goal of providing information that is as accurate and as reliable as possible. Regardless, purchasing this eBook can be seen as consent to the fact that both the publisher and the author of this book are in no way experts on the topics discussed within, and that any recommendations or suggestions made herein are for entertainment purposes only. Professionals should be consulted as needed before undertaking any of the action endorsed herein.

This declaration is deemed fair and valid by both the American Bar Association and the Committee of Publishers Association and is legally binding throughout the United States.

Furthermore, the transmission, duplication or reproduction of any of the following work, including precise information, will be considered an illegal act, irrespective whether it is done electronically or in print. The legality extends to creating a secondary or tertiary copy of the work or a recorded copy and is only allowed with express written consent of the Publisher. All additional rights are reserved.

The information in the following pages is broadly considered to be a truthful and accurate account of facts, and as such any inattention, use or misuse of the information in question by the reader will render any resulting actions solely under their purview. There are no scenarios in which the publisher or the original author of this work can be in any fashion deemed liable for any hardship or damages that may befall them after undertaking information described herein.

Additionally, the information found on the following pages is intended for informational purposes only and should thus be considered, universal. As befitting its nature, the information presented is without assurance regarding its continued validity or interim quality. Trademarks that mentioned are done without written consent and can in no way be considered an endorsement from the trademark holder.

Table of Contents

Introduction 1

Chapter 1: What is Google Classroom? 3

Chapter 2: Managing Your Own Google Classroom 16

Chapter 3: Using Google Classroom as a Teacher..................... 20

Chapter 4: FAQS About Google Classroom 31

Chapter 5: Other Ways Google Classroom Can Help Teachers in the Classroom 35

Conclusion.. 39

Introduction

Congratulations on downloading your personal copy of *Google Classroom: Teacher Guide to Google Classroom.* Thank you for doing so.

Google Classroom is one of the best online resources that you can use to bring your classroom to the next level. This platform allows you to interact with your students, send out emails, work on assignments and discussions and so much more. As a teacher, you will appreciate all of the things that you are able to do with the help of Google Classroom. This guidebook will take some time to go over Google Classroom and what you can do with this amazing tool.

Some of the things that we will discuss in this guidebook pertaining to Google Classroom includes:

- What is Google Classroom?
- How to manage your own Google Classroom
- How to use Google Classroom as a teacher
- FAQS about Google Classroom
- Other ways Google Classroom can help teachers in the classroom.

Google Classroom is a free tool that students and teachers can use to bring together learning in a new and fun way. Check out this guidebook to learn how to get started in no time!

The following chapters will discuss some of the many of the things that you need to know in order to make Google Classroom work for your needs. This is the ultimate teacher's guide, the information that you need in order to take Google Classroom and make it enhance what you are teaching in the traditional classroom. There is so much that you can do with the help of Google Classroom to get the results that you would like.

This guidebook is going to take a look at all of the things that you are able to do with the help of Google Classroom. You will learn some of the benefits that come with Google Classroom, how to set up your own account and your own classes, how to add students and teachers to the classroom, and so much more. Teachers will enjoy how they are able to interact with their students, share information, send out assignments and announcements that are needed. This is a fantastic way to help teachers and students to interact with each other and to ensure that each student is learning in the way that is right for them.

If you are a teacher and you would like to find some new ways to interact with your students and to personalize the learning experience for your class, read through this guidebook and learn what you need to know to make Google Classroom work for you!

There are plenty of books on this subject on the market, thanks again for choosing this one! Every effort was made to ensure it is full of as much useful information as possible. Please enjoy!

Chapter 1: What is Google Classroom?

Thanks to all of the advances in technology that have occurred in the past few decades, there are now many different ways that you will be able to work with your students to create a great learning environment. You are not stuck with a one size fits all when it comes to the classroom and you can add in some other good things like links, documents, videos, and more that you may not have had access to in the past. Some of these options will help you to save time in the classroom while still providing your students with a personalized learning approach that can't be found anywhere else.

Think of how much time it takes to hand out an assignment, repeat the instructions a few times, hope that you get all of the assignments back, hear excuses about why it is late, correct it all, and then move on to the next topic? This is all going to take up a lot of your time, plus you are going to miss out on providing students with individualized attention or a good explanation of why they got certain things wrong. There just isn't time to get all of this done in the traditional classroom and some students are going to end up falling behind because they just don't understand what is going on.

Thanks to all of the great technology that is going on in the world around us, you can solve many of these issues. You can use emails to correspond with students and explain what they did wrong inside their assignments, even if they are too shy to discuss this in the class. You can keep the instructions and all of the assignments online so no one is able to lose them or they can look up the instructions and ask questions all at the same time. You can make it so that the system grades the papers for you instantly to save even more time.

One of the best systems that you are able to use in your

classroom, whether you are looking to use it to enhance your in-person classroom or to replace it completely, is Google Classroom. Google Classroom is a blended learning platform that can be used in schools. The aim of this platform is to simply creating, distributing, and even grading assignments in a paperless way. This was a platform that was introduced as part of the Google Apps for Education when it was publicly released in August of 2014.

The aim of Google Classroom is to help teachers and students to interact in a new way so that both are able to make the learning experience much more enjoyable. The teacher will be able to create assignments, send out announcements, and post other useful information for the students to look over. They can also watch for group discussions, answer questions, and more to make this a more effective method of teaching without taking up too much time in the classroom.

There are many different parts that students and teachers alike are going to enjoy when it comes to the Google Classroom. You will be able to utilize the Spreadsheets, Calendar to keep track of all the assignments, Gmail, Forms, and so much more. As the teacher, you will be able to choose which features of the Google Classroom you would like to work with to enhance what you are teaching inside of your classroom.

What Google Classroom Does

One of the first questions that you may have about Google Classroom is what this platform is going to be able to do with this. There are quite a few different platforms that are similar to this one so you may be curious as to how this one is going to be the best option for you compared to the other ones. Not only are you going to get some of the great features that come with Google and what you are familiar with, which is one of the main benefits that you will see when working in Google Classroom.

Luckily, there are quite a few different things that you will be able to work with when working in Google Classroom. Some of the things that Google Classroom will be able to help you do include:

- Using Gmail at school. As a teacher, you will be able to create your own Gmail account. From there, you can search for any important messages or ones that are school related. You won't have to worry about the ads or any other delays that are common with some of the other email services. Gmail is one that many people are familiar with so you will be happy to use this more often.
- As a teacher, you will find that working with Google Classroom is going to help you to streamline your class. You will be able to do this by creating your assignments, being able to share your assignments and announcements with ease, and you can even grade them without wasting a lot of time.
- It is easy for both the teachers and the students to work together through docs. You will be able to create as well as edit various presentations, docs, and spreadsheets inside of your browser. In addition, you are able to do all of this while making sure that all of the changes are saved automatically. It is also possible for more than one person to work on something at the same time without having any issues.
- Your students will be able to share their work, as well as save their work, all on the cloud. This makes it easier for them to access the files whenever they want, even if they are not at home. This can be helpful for you as the teacher as well because you can upload some information to the cloud as well for your students to get ahold of. This helps save some of the hassle and the time that comes with sending attachments or merging together the different versions.
- The Google Calendar is a great option to use with the Google Classroom. Calendars in here are able to be

shared. This makes it easier to plan for projects and you can also integrate together with your hangouts, contacts, email accounts, and Google Drive.

- As the teacher, you are going to find that using Google Calendars can be great. You can put up an announcement or an assignment and give it a due date. Then this due date and assignment are going to show up on the class page for all of the students that are linked to this classroom. You won't have to constantly update students about when a due date is about to come. They just need to take a look at their own Calendar to find out this information.
- If you feel that you need to set up a website that you are able to use for your class, Google Classroom is able to help out. This is something that you could do for a specific project or event or you can set it up so that the students are able to create some of their own websites as well.
- If it is needed, you are able to conduct meetings that are face to face with the help of video calls to your students. This can be really efficient if a student has a quick question that they would like to have answered. Some teachers have been able to use this service in order to create their own virtual field trip.
- Sometimes the chats and the emails can get all over the place and there are going to be too many of them. The teacher is able to archive these emails and these chats so that they can go through them at a later time if you would like. It is also really easy to organize your emails and chats so it is easier for you to use.
- It is possible to use some of the different add-on apps that you need to make more happen within the class. You could use Google+, Blogger, and Google Groups to make the class a bit more productive than you can in a traditional classroom.

These are just a few of the things that you are able to do when working within Google Classroom. As the teacher, you are able to pick out the things that you want to do inside the classroom, and each class is going to be a little bit different. It is completely fine to mix and match things together to make them personalized for the class that you are teaching.

How is Google Classroom different than a personal account?

As a teacher, you may be curious as to why you would want to go with Google Classroom rather than working with your personal account. It is possible to work with your personal account in the classroom, but you do not get the results that you are looking for. For example, with a personal account, you will have to worry about sending through bulky emails if you are sending out attachments. The due dates that you pick are not going to upload to Google Calendars, and information can easily get lost for students if it isn't all put in the same place.

It is possible to work with your own personal account, but in reality, Google Classroom is one of the best options to help you to manage your classroom. This platform is all about being used for educational purposes. It doesn't cost anything to get started and it can save most teachers around 52 hours of work time each year, which is nothing to sneeze at. Add in that Google Classroom rarely experiences any downtime and they have a great customer support system, and this is one of the best options for you to go with.

If you just want to send a few emails back and forth between your students and you aren't interested in moving any of your classrooms online, your personal account with Gmail is probably going to be just fine. On the other hand, if you are interested in moving some or a lot of your classroom online and you want to make sure that it is a platform that is really easy for your students to get on and use, then Google Classroom is the right option for you.

Getting the Google Classroom app

Before you are able to make Google Classroom a part of your teaching experience, you need to make sure that you download the Google Apps for Education. This is a pretty simple process to go through and have work for you, but there are a few steps that you will need to work on first.

First, there are a few rules for who is able to get on the Google Classroom app. Any student, parent or alumni group that has been registered as a 501(c)(3) can get on the Google Classroom app. Also, any accredited or non-profit K through 12 learning institutions can use this as well. You may want to consider talking to your administrator to see if this is a service that is already offered through your school or not.

Once you have checked in on this part, you will need to go through the following steps in order to sign up for the app:

- You will want to start by going to the sign-up form for the Apps for Education. You will be able to find it at https://www.google.com/a/signup/u/0/?enterprise_product=GOOGLE.EDU#0
- Once you are on this page, you can fill the form in and then click on the Next button.
- From here, you will provide your institution's domain. If this isn't available, you can go through and purchase a new domain to help you get this started.
- Then click on Next and provide the rest of the information that is needed so that you can become an admin.
- Make sure to read through the Agreement before accepting and finishing the sign-up.

You may want to consider doing this a little bit early, like before school starts, because it can take up to two weeks before Google is done reviewing the application. After this time frame, you are going to receive your own acceptance form when the application is successful. You will now be able to verify your own domain as well as add addresses, mail integration, apps, and contacts to start using this. Keep in mind that you will not need to do this for each class, but you only need to go through this and do it one time. Once you are in, you will be able to assign different classrooms and have more than one in place under the same account.

From here, you will need to work on downloading the Google Classroom App. You will be able to go to the App Store and get this one just by looking for Google Classroom, or you can just visit Google Play and find it as well. Once you have downloaded this particular app, you will need to choose to sign in as the teacher. It is also possible to download an extension or a bookmark-like app that will work on Google Chrome. You just need to go visit Chrome Store in order to install all of this.

There are a few ways that you are able to install the Google Classroom App so that you can use it for your own needs. If you are considered the administrator, you will be able to install this extension by using the following steps:

- Visit the Google Admin Console
- From here you will click on Chrome Management and then User Settings
- Then you will be able to select the organizational unit that you would like to work with from here.
- Now you can click on Apps & Extension before clicking on Force Installed Apps & Extension. When you get to this point, click on Manage Force Installed App.
- Inside of this tab, you will click on Chrome Web Store and then look for the series of letters that don't seem to make sense and click on those. If you can't find that, you can click on Share to Classroom.
- Now click the Add button that is right next to your

extension before hitting save.

These steps are only if you are going to be the administrator. If you are using the Google Classroom through your educational institution, you will not need to go through the steps above because someone else will go through and do it. The steps that you will need to go through as a teacher, and that your students will need to go through as well, include:

- Visit g.co/sharetoclassroom
- When you get here, you can click on Add to Chrome and then click on the Add button
- From here you can click on the icon that is next to the extension. You will need to make sure that you are signed in with Google before you do all of this.

And that is all that you will need to do to make sure that Google Classroom is downloaded for you and that you are able to use it for your classroom and your teaching experience. Since this is such a popular platform to work with, it is likely that your school already has this available for you to use for your classes or they will be interested in learning more about it.

The Classroom Screen Reader

Another thing that you may want to use when you are working with Google Classroom is the Google Classroom Screen Reader. This is a great tool that will help teachers to stay organized in a way that they would not have been able to do in the past. In order to use the Classroom Screen Reader, you will use the following steps:

- First, you will need to sign in to classroom.google.com and select that you are the teacher.
- From here you can go to the Classroom Menu before pressing Enter.
- Then you are able to navigate to any of the classes that you would like and even spend some time to manage your

preferences.

And that is all that you will need to do to make this work for your classroom. Each teacher is going to find that there are different features of Google Classroom that end up working the best for them, so spend some time looking around and learning as much as you can about this great education platform before getting started.

Advantages of using Google Classroom over another educational platform

There are really so many advantages that you will love when working with Google Classroom and many teachers have already chosen to go with this platform to help them to get the most out of their work and to save time while still providing a personalized learning experience for their students. Some of the great benefits that you will be able to enjoy with the help of Google Classroom includes:

Easy to access

Even if you or one of your students are not a big Google user, it is still easy to work with the Google Classroom. Since this platform is delivered with the help of the Chrome browser, which already makes it really accessible from all tablets, phones, and computers, it is easy for the teacher to add in as many learners, or students, as they would like. The teacher is also able to use Google Classroom to create some Google documents, to manage their announcements and assignments, to post on YouTube videos, and to even attach files with the help of Google Drive. Users, such as the students, will find it really easy to log into this kind of classroom as well as receive their assignments and turn these assignments in.

Effective for sharing and communication

One of the biggest advantages that you will find with Google

Classroom is the ability to use Google Docs. These are documents that can be saved online while also being shared with as many people as you would like. This means that when a teacher creates a new assignment or announcement with Google Docs, they are able to send it out and the students can access it right away in the Google Drive, as long as this folder has been shared with them. Google Docs also have methods to help organize and personalize all the folders in the Google Drive. You no longer need to spend all that time sharing that information through emails, you can just work on a document and then share it with as many of the students in the class that you need.

Speeds up the process of assignments

Google Classroom makes it possible to create a new assignment and then distribute it to all of the students in a classroom with just one click. Then students are able to work on the assignment and then turn it in almost instantly based on how long it takes them to complete it. This really streamlines the whole assignment process because as the teacher, you will be able to easily check which students have submitted the assignment, who is working on it, and more. The teacher can also take a look at the assignment and provide some feedback right away.

Effective feedback

In a traditional classroom, it is really hard to provide all of the students with the feedback they need. All of the students could be asking questions at the same time or you just don't have the minutes needed to do it in class. You can use Google Classroom to provide the right online support to your students immediately. This helps the feedback to be effective because it will include some of your recent comments and your students are able to ask questions and get things clarified if needed.

Saves on paper

Instead of having to print off a lot of different papers for the assignments and then having to grade all of these, you can put everything on Google Classroom. This not only speeds up the process a little bit, but it helps to save you a lot when it comes to the amount of paper that you are going to use. It helps you to save time and paper because you no longer need to worry about printing off the assignments that you need to use or even handing them out. Gone are the days when your students will be able to lose all of their homework and you need to print more off because it is all online now.

Easy to use interface

If you have used any of the Google products in the past, you are probably used to seeing the clean layout standards that are pretty common with any of the other Google platforms. Google Classroom stays pretty loyal to this. The environment that is found in Google Classroom is full of simple, user-friendly, and intuitive design details. For teachers, as well as students, who are familiar with using Google or any of their other options, Google Classroom is going to feel very familiar and easy to use.

Commenting system

Inside of Google Classroom, your students are going to be able to comment right at a specific location, such as within the pictures, for some of their online courses so you won't have to search around to find what they are meaning. IN addition, you are able to create a URL for interesting comments and then use these for some of your further online discussions if you would like.

Everyone can use it

Teachers are able to use Google Classroom not just with their students, but with other teachers inside the same institution. Educators would end up joining this as learners and then the Google Classroom would be used for information sharing, personal development, and faculty meetings. If your educational institution wants to work in this manner, it is possible to do, you would just need to get the link to sign up in this manner. This is a great way for educators throughout the same system to share ideas, get together, and learn how to better their profession all at the same time.

While there are a lot of things that you are going to love when it comes to using Google Classroom, but there are a few disadvantages that you need to be aware of. To start with, Google Classroom is going to be very familiar to some of the other Google platforms that you have used. For those who are familiar with Gmail and some of the other options from Google, this is not a big deal, but if you have a student who hasn't used any of these in the past, it can become a little bit confusing.

If you are worried that some of your students are unfamiliar with how to use the Google programs, you may want to consider setting up a little tutorial for them to follow. You can have that available as a resource for anyone to check out if they need, or you can make that one of the first assignments to make sure that everyone ends up on the same page.

Another thing that you can keep in mind when creating your own class is that Google Classroom is not able to provide you with automated tests and quizzes for the students who are in your class. Right now, Google Classroom is considered to be the best for a blended learning experience, rather than for one that is fully online. This means that it is going to work the best for those classes that usually meet in person but who want to use some of the services and benefits outside of class time as well.

The good news is there are some apps that you are able to use that can help with this process. You can add them into the Google Classroom to help with grading and leave remarks for your students. These are still being worked on so you may have to just do the quizzes and tests in a different way when you are first getting started. But if you are just looking to provide some better feedback to your students, to have your assignments and announcements all in one place, and to have a good way to interact with your students outside the classroom, Google Classroom is the best option for you.

Some people have even complained that the interface and the use of Google Classroom are not as personal as some of the others, but you are able to go in and add some different color schemes and themes to your page to make it a bit better. There are some limitations on what you are able to do right now, but Google is always expanding out to provide more options for their users.

There are many reasons that you will want to work with Google Classrooms to make learning more enjoyable for all of the students you are working with. This is not a system that will work for everyone, but since it is easy to get started with, fun to use, and can work for everyone while also being free, it is a choice that many teachers are choosing to go with.

Chapter 2: Managing Your Own Google Classroom

Now that you have your Google Classroom App ready to go, it is time to learn how to manage some of your classes. The Google Classroom API is going to be the part that will make the features of your Google Classroom work. This part is going to let schools, as well as technological companies, work in order to create all of the apps that the teachers will need to communicate with the students who are in their classes so they can get the best learning experience possible.

You will find that managing your Google Classroom is going to be pretty easy to work with. You will be able to list out the different assignments that you want to work with, making sure that you put them in the right classes if you have more than one, and your students will be able to work from there. You also don't have to worry about students knowing when due dates are; your assignments will automatically update the due date onto Google Calendars for the students, saving you a lot of time and hassle in the process.

There are so many things that you are able to do when it comes to managing your own Google Classroom. Some teachers will just use this to post up the announcements and others some assignments, but there are some who recognize all the value that you are able to get with Google Classroom, and they will use it to manage their classes even more. There are so much that you will be able to do with this platform, from opening up discussions, sharing links, offering feedback, and so much more. Let's take a look at some of the basics that you are able to do in order to manage your Google Classroom.

Managing the Courses

When you are inside of Google Classroom, a course is going to be one class. As a teacher, you will be able to host more than one class; as many of these as you would need to make it through each semester or each year. You may want to take some time to add a few details into the name of each class to make sure that you are able to recognize which one is right and to ensure that you put each student into the right spot as well. For example, instead of just putting in "Physics" for a class, especially if you have several classes that are Physics. You may want to call it something like Advanced Physics I, 4th Period, to keep things in line.

Inside each of the classes, you are going to be able to find a lot of different things that will help you to get more done with each of your courses. You will be able to find the metadata for all of the classes, the students that you invite to the class, and then the teachers. You are able to add in another teacher to help you with the course if you would like. It also supports

- Domain: the domain is going to be important because without having this in place, you will have trouble with creating the addresses and aliases that you would like. If these were not in place, you and the students will not know what parts you are able to use inside of the Google Classroom.
- Developer project: this is the part that will help you to manage all of your aliases or the names that you give to your different applications. You will be able to see that these get tied to the Google's Console Developer's Project.

Managing as an Administrator

In some cases, you will be the administrator if you set up your own Google Classroom Account and it is important to learn how to work in this capacity. In other cases, your educational institution will have someone else be the administrator and you will just be one of the teachers who has the option to make changes and create classrooms on the app.

The Google Classroom API is going to help the administrator to know the difference between the student and the teachers. There are sometimes when the person could be a teacher as well as a student based on what is going on in the course, but for the most part, one person is going to be the teacher of the class and the rest will be the students and each will have different options for what they are allowed to do inside of the different classes. The differences between teachers and students in Google Classroom include:

- Teachers: the teachers are going to be the people who will be in charge of instructing and running a certain course. These are the people who will be allowed to view as well as change any of the details of the course. They are also going to be responsible for managing all of the students in the course and they will control the flow of the course.
- Students: in order to complete the course, you will need to have some students in it. These are all the other people who enroll in the class. They will get to see the teachers who are in the class and some of the course details that the teacher adds in.

The teacher will be able to determine who gets to be in their particular class. They can choose to ask students at the beginning of the year for the preferred emails for contact. The teacher will be able to send out a link to the particular classroom and the students can click on it and see what is available inside the class. The teacher can also create a code and hand it out to the students who will be able to add this in to find the classes that they need to be in.

In addition, all of the users in the class are able to add in as well as customize a Share Button that is able to be used in order to meet the needs of anyone else who is accessing the website. This is a good button to use when you would like to add on blogs or websites so that it is easier for others to access and share it. The administrator of your Google Classroom Account will be able to determine how the Share Button looks and how big it can be. This can help to provide some more traffic to the website as well.

The teacher is going to have a lot of control over how they are able to manage their classrooms, they just need to have the right permissions to get into the classroom and then they need to invite all of the right students so everyone is on the right page. There are quite a few other things that the teacher is able to do with their own Google Classroom, but getting it all set up is one of the first steps.

Chapter 3: Using Google Classroom as a Teacher

As the teacher, there are a lot of different things that you will be able to do when using Google Classroom. This tool can be as simple or as complex as you would like. Some teachers just use this to send a few emails and post their announcements, but this is really a way to save you a lot of time and energy while still making sure that you are giving all of the students a personalized education at the same time. From providing instant feedback to some of the work that you give to the students to emailing, setting up group discussions, and so much more, Google Classroom is going to become one of your best friends when it is time to get things done.

If you are the teacher and you want to work with Google Classroom for your teaching, you will need to make sure that you start with creating your own class. You will have to make a new class for all of the subjects and time periods that you are teaching because you don't want to have people becoming confused by shoving all that information, especially for different subjects, inside of the same class. The steps are pretty easy though and you will happy with how quickly you are able to get several classes set up. Let's look at some of the steps that you can take to add in a class and get your classrooms all set up!

Adding in a class

The first step that you will need to work on is adding in a class. You will need to do the following steps for each of the classes that you are going to teach for the year, but since they are pretty simple to set up, you won't have a lot of work to do. In order to add one of your first classes in Google Classroom, you would use the following steps if working inside of a web browser:

- Go to classroom.google.com and then sign in with your credentials.
- Click on the (+) sign, and then on Create Class.
- Look around to see the first empty text box and then place in the name that you would like to name the class.
- Under the name of the class, you will want to add in a short description. There should be a second text box for you to be able to do this. You can also add in the section, the grade level, or the class time to make it easier to find the class.
- When all of this is set up, you will just need to click on the create button to get the class started.

The steps above are all about working on a web browser on your personal computer. If you would like to use your iOS device to set up the class, you would use the following steps.

- Go to your classroom.google.com account and then click on the icon that kind of looks like a person.
- From here, you can click on, or use your fingers, the (+) sign and then click on Create Class.
- From here you will need to add in the information for the class that you are working on. You can enter the name of the class as well as a small description of the class in your second box.
- When all of the right information is inside of the boxes, you can click on Create and your class is ready.

You can also choose to set up one of these classrooms with the help of your Android device. Some of the steps that you can take to use your Android device includes:

- Go to the classroom.google.com and use your credentials in order to sign in.
- Look for the icon that looks like a person and click on that to start.

- Touch on the (+) sign and then push Create Class.
- Enter the name of the class as well as the description and the other information that you would like to use in the second box.
- When all of this is in the right place, you can click on create and then your class is all ready to go.

Adding in a Resource Page to the Class

Now that the class is all set up to use, it is time to add some substance to your class, some information that the students will be able to use to get the information that they need about this class. A class resource page is a good place to start because it is the place where you will be able to post some of your instructional materials. This could include some information about grading policies, classroom rules, lessons, and even your syllabus.

This should be a place where you spend some time letting the students know what they can expect when they come onto the page and need to work in your class. Some of the things that you can do to set up the class resource page include:

- Go to your classroom.google.com page.
- Choose the class that you want to use in order to add in a resource page if you have more than one class.
- From here you will click on the About button on the top of the page.
- You can then pick out a title and a description for your class from here.
- In the Room Field, add in a location and then leave it blank.
- Click on Add Materials to add the different resources that you want to use in the classroom. For example, if the teacher wants to attach a specific file, they will be able to click on the right icon. Then they can locate the item that they want to use and click on Add. If you don't need to

- add on an attachment, just click on X.
- Once all of the attachments are placed in the resource page you can click on Post, and then make sure to save as well.

You can always go back through and add in more resources through the year if you would like. You can start out with some of the information that the students need at the beginning of the year and then add in some more information if this works out the best for your class. There are no limits to what you are able to do with your resource page so have some fun and add in the information that your students will need to succeed in the class.

Add in other teachers

It is also possible to add in other teachers to the Classroom as well to make learning a bit more enjoyable. If you have another teacher who is working on the same kind of lesson plans, both of you can share the account and share information between your students. This will make it easier for both of you to work together, answer questions, and get more done inside of the classroom. In addition, if you have a student teacher or someone else who is working together in the traditional classroom with you, it is a good idea to add them in with teacher privileges in the classroom as well.

When you are ready to add in some more teachers to the Google Classroom, no matter what the reason may be, you will need to go with the following steps to make this happen:

- Go in and sign in to your classroom.google.com account.
- You can then go and pick out the class that you would like to add in another teacher or two to, and then click on the About button that is on the top of the screen.
- Here you should see a button that says Invite Teacher. Click on that and then put a check mark into the box that is next to the teachers you would like to invite. They will

already need to be in the Google Classroom system for your institution for you to be able to do this.
- If you decide to add in everyone who is on the list, you are able to click on Select All to make this happen.
- If you notice that one of the teachers that you would like to invite is not on this list, you will just need to click on My Contacts and then follow the steps above again.

Adding in other teachers to your classroom can be a great way to share some of the work, get someone to help you out with a larger class, and even to enhance some of the learning experience for all of the students. There are a few things that you should notice about adding in teachers to your classroom though. To start, the class can only be deleted by the teacher who is considered primary on the account. So if you set up the class, you will be the only one who can delete the class. The primary teacher can also not be un-enrolled or removed from the class. This is because the primary teacher is going to be the one that owns all of the materials that belong to the class, such as the structures, folders, assignments and more and if this primary teacher were taken off the class, the system would not work properly.

If there is a teacher who is in the class, you are not able to mute them. This means that they will be able to make comments, leave feedback and more when they are in the classroom. You should make sure that everyone is on the same page for how they are supposed to behave in the class because it will be hard to stop behavior without removing the teacher completely from the class later on.

When your email notifications are on, the primary and the additional teachers are all going to be notified of the comments that the students send in, even if these comments are private. However, you can change this a little bit and ask the students to send an email directly to you, rather than through the messaging system, to make it more private if they would like.

When there are other teachers in the system, they are also able to add in some more materials to the classroom to help with the learning experience. If they do add in some new materials, all of these materials are going to be found in the primary teacher's folder.

Inviting in the students

Now that you have spent some time getting the Google Classroom all setup, it is time to add in the students. It is not going to be much of a classroom if all you have there are some of the teachers. There are a few ways that you are able to add in the students who should be in the class and you are able to choose the one that works for you. Remember that you will need to go through these steps for each of the classes that you set up, so be careful that you are getting the right students into the right classes. Also, before setting this up you should remember that all of the classes on Google Classroom will have a maximum of 20 teachers and 1000 students at one time, but this is often going to be way more than you will need for your classes.

As mentioned, there are a few different methods that you can use in order to get some students into your Classroom. The first method we are going to take a look at just inviting the students to come joins the class. To do this, you would use the following steps:

Go to your classroom.google.com account.

From here, you will want to work on adding the students to the class that you have chosen. So go into the chosen class and then click on Students and then Invite.

- Tick on the box next to all of the names of the students that you need to add into the class. If all of the students on the list need to be invited you can click on Select All.
- If you need to see some other lists to get the students that you would like to add in, you would need to click on My

Contacts. You can also click on Directory to see some of the other students who are in your domain.
- When your list is all done, you are able to click on Invite students.

This is going to send out an invite to all of your students. They will be able to click on the link and then be added to the Classroom that you set up. You can also choose to give your students a code. You would come up with a code for the class and then the students will be able to go in and add themselves to the class. Some of the steps that you would need to do to give out the code to the classroom include:

- Go to your classroom.google.com account.
- From here, you will need to get into the class page at the bottom of the stream. Here you should be able to find the email addresses for the students here.
- Send out an email to all of the students from there with the code inside so that they can use this to join the class. You can also choose to write down the code and give it to the students in class.
- You will want to let the students know that they will be able to sign into the classroom by visiting classroom.google.com and then click on the (+) sign before entering the code that you give them and pressing on Join.
- You will then be able to disable or reset the code as you need.

At this point, the students should be able to get into your classroom and see the information that you put there. You can also choose to invite students that are on a particular Google Group. The steps that you would need to make this happen include:

- Go to your classroom.google.com account.
- You can add in the students that you want with the class

and then click on the Students button on the top.
- From here you will want to click on Students, then Invite, and then My Contact.
- You can then select the particular Google Group that you would like to use in order to invite people from.
- Here you can add a tick to the box that is next to the name of the student that you need to add to this class. You can also choose to click on Select All if it is easier for you and you want to add in all of the students.
- When that is done, you can click on Invite Students and the invitation will be sent out.

All of these options are going to work well to help you get your first Google Classroom all setup and it will ensure that all of the students get the invite that they need to become a part of the class. You can choose any of the options that work the best for your needs or for your class, but they can all be great options to help you out. Make sure to get those students invited so you can start sharing information with them, giving out assignments, and providing answers and feedback to help your students learn more than before.

Setting the permissions for the class

As a teacher, it is going to be up to you to decide what is going to happen inside of your classroom. You will need to go through and set up the permissions for the Classroom to make sure that everything goes the way that you would like. There are many different permissions that you are able to set up out, but first, we are going to take a look at the post and comment permissions. To set these, you would use the following steps:

- Go into the Classroom page for the class you are working on and click on Students.
- From here you can click on Students can Post and Comment. You can then tweak how this works, but there are a few things that you should keep in mind:

- Students can post and comment: if you click on this one, it means that the students are able to make posts as well as comments when they would like. If you are choosing this one, you should make sure to set out some ground rules for what is allowed with posting to keep things in order.
- Students can comment only: this means that the student will be able to add in the comments that they want, but they are not able to start their own posts. If you are working on a discussion question, you are able to just have the students comment if that is easier.
- Only the teacher can post or comment: this means that you do not want to allow the students to post or comment on this in any way. This is usually not one that you would want to use since Google Classroom works the best when you are able to communicate with each other.

Another thing that you may want to consider is to mute the students. If you find that the students are getting a bit out of control, aren't contributing in a positive way to the discussion or something else, you may want to choose to mute them for a bit. The steps that you are able to take to make this happen includes:

- Click on students
- You can then look for the names of the students that you wish to mute, and then click on the box that is next to their name. you can choose to mute just one or two students or all of them if needed.
- You need to click on Actions and then Mute before clicking on Mute again.
- You can also mute students while they are comments. You can look under the comments section and then click on the class where the student you would like to mute is from.

- You can then Find the said comments before selecting Mute the Student name.
- From here you will click on Mute.
- You can also choose to delete the particular comment if needed. All you need to do for that is click delete, which is right there by the comment, before leaving.

If you have deleted a post or a comment while running the class and you would like to see it again, this is also a possibility. You will just need to click the X which is under the Stream part of the page. You can then click on the Check Mark that is there to hide the deleted items if you are all done with them.

Removing a Student or a Teacher

There are some times when you will want to delete a teacher or a student from the Classroom. If the teacher was just there to help with a certain lesson, a student dropped out of the class, or you ended up adding the wrong person to the mix, this is something that you will need to do. To start with, we are going to look at the steps that you need to take in order to delete the teacher. To do this, you would need to:

- Click on the About part of the classroom that you are in. You can then look for the name of the teacher before clicking on Remove From Class.
- To work with the students, you would need to click on the Students Tab. Look through this to find the name of the student that you would like to remove.
- From here, click on Actions and then click Remove.
- You will need to click on Remove again to confirm that you would like to remove the student.

Viewing the Class Calendar

As a teacher, you are going to appreciate the Calendar and how it is going to keep things together inside of your classroom. When you post up announcements, tests and other things that have due dates on them, you will see that the Google Calendar will collect this information and put it on for everyone to be able to see. If you would like to take a look at your own calendar to make sure that everything is in order the right way, you would just need to use the following steps:

- Click on Calendar when you are in the Classroom page.
- Then you can click on an assignment that is on your Calendar, or you can click on Quick Question in order to access the information from the Student page if needed.
- You can click on the arrow next to know what is going on or this week or even the following week so you can plan out your time.
- If you would like to be able to filter out the events, you can click on the All Classes button, and then choose which class you need to have a filter of events for.

This Calendar is going to make it easier for all of your students to know when homework is due and when they need to get things handed in by. It can save you a lot of hassle in the long run because you will not have to remind your students about these due dates; they are able to just view it on their Calendar and have it all in one place.

As you can see, there are a lot of things that you are able to do as a teacher through Google Classroom. Setting up the classes may take a little bit of time, but it is going to help you to keep organized and to get the things done that you need. Once each of the classes is set up and you invite in the students that you need to make it work, you are able to send over links, work on assignments, and provide the feedback that they need to really learn at their own rate and get the most out of the classroom. This is really a great way to make your classroom more personalized and easier for everyone to use, and as you can see, it doesn't take too much work to get it all setup!

Chapter 4: FAQS About Google Classroom

As a teacher, there are a lot of different options that you can use to make the most out of your classroom and you may be curious as to why Google Classroom is the best option to help you out. There are many questions that you may have that pertain to Google Classroom. Some of the questions that you may have about Google Classroom include:

Is it easy to get started with Google Classroom?

Yes, it is really easy to work with Google Classroom, but you do need to remember that it is necessary to have the Google Apps for Education and your domain needs to be verified. We discussed how to do this a little bit how to get the Google Apps for Education as well as setting up your domain so make sure that you follow these instructions so that the application can be reviewed right from the beginning.

How are Apps for Education and Classroom connected?

To keep things simple, Google Classroom is not able to work without the help of Google Apps for Education. While you are able to use the Apps for Education all on its own, you will find that using Google Classroom is going to help to make all of it organized and it is much easier to work with. With the help of both the Classroom and Apps working together, both the students and the teachers are able to access the spreadsheets, slideshows, and documents as well as other links without having to worry about attachments and more. Even giving and receiving assignments and grades are easier when these two are combined together.

In addition, there is the option to download the Classroom Mobile app, which will make it easier to access your classes whenever and wherever you would like. This is going to be great for students who are on the go and don't have time to always look through their laptop to see announcements. Even teachers are able to use this mobile app to help them get up assignments and announcements when they are on the go so they can concentrate on other thanks later on.

Does it cost to use Google Classroom?

One of the best things about using Google Classroom is that it is completely free. All you need is a bit of time to help get it all setup, but it will not include any out of pocket costs to make it work. You will have to wait about two weeks in the beginning for your application to be reviewed before you are able to use the class, so consider setting this up early to prevent issues with falling behind.

You will never have to pay for anything when you are using Google Classroom. If you run into a vendor who is asking for you to pay for Google Classroom, you should report them to Google. It is highly likely that this is a fake vendor so do not work with them or provide them with any of your payment information. Google Classroom is, and always will be, free for you to use.

Can I still use Classroom if it is disabled on my domain?

One of the nice things about working with Classroom is that even if it has been disabled on a certain domain, you are still able to use it. With that being said, there are going to be a few restrictions. While you may still be able to get access to a lot of the features, such as Google Drive, Google Docs, and Gmail, you may not be able to see some of the slides, docs, and sheets that were saved in the classroom. It is always best to have your domain turned on when you are working in Google Classroom because this ensures that you are able to use all of the features that are available through the Classroom.

Do I need to have Gmail enabled to use classroom?

It is not necessary to have Gmail enabled in order to use the Google Classroom. You are able to use the Classroom as much as you would like without enabling Gmail, but you would find that you wouldn't be able to receive notifications if the Gmail account isn't turned on. If you would like to have some notifications sent to you, you need to have Gmail enabled.

If you are not that fond of using the Gmail account for this, it is possible to set up your own email server to make it work. This way, you will still be able to receive the notifications that are needed from the Classroom while using the email server that you like the most.

Will I have to work with ads on Google Classroom?

Many people like to work with Google Classroom because they don't have to worry about seeing ads all over the place. Classroom was designed for educational purposes, and Google recognizes that people don't want to have to fight with ads all of the time when they are learning. You can rest assured that Google and Classroom are not going to take your information and use it for advertising. This is part of the privacy and security that is offered with Google Classroom, which will protect both the student and the teacher from any phishing or spam.

If I have a disability, am I able to use Google Classroom?

Yes, those with disabilities are able to use Google Classroom.

Some of the features are not yet complete, but Google is working to make some improvements to classroom so that those who have disabilities can use it too. Aside from using the Screen reader, there are a few other features that you can use with Android including:

- BrailleBack: this is a great feature that is going to allow for Braille to be displayed on the Android Device, as long as you have your Bluetooth installed. This is also going to work with the Screen Reader feature that we talked about before. With this feature, you will also be able to input your text while interacting with your Android device.
- Switch Access: it is also possible for you to use Switch Access, which is a tool that allows you to control your device with two or more switches. This is great for those who are dealing with limited mobility. It is also a good way to get notifications and alerts.

You are also able to tweak some of the settings that are in Google Classroom in regards to color correction, magnification, captions, touch and hold, using a speaking password, and more.

As you can see, there are a lot of neat things that you are able to do when it comes to using Google Classroom and it is pretty easy for everyone to be able to use. If you ever have some other questions about Google Classroom, you can always contact their support to get the assistance that you need.

Chapter 5: Other Ways Google Classroom Can Help Teachers in the Classroom

Teachers are going to love all of the features that they are able to use when it comes to using Google Classroom. They can choose to use the Classroom just a little bit or use it to really integrate into the traditional classroom and get so much more out of the whole experience. In this guidebook, we have spent some time talking about a lot of the different things that you can do when you bring Google Classroom into your learning experience. But there is still so much more that you are able to do. Some of the other neat things that you will be able to do with the help of Google Classroom includes:

- Sharing resources: it is easy to share some of the resources that you have through Google Classroom. You can pick to share a link share a video, share documents, and so much more in one location.
- Create a new lesson: you are not stuck with just assigning some work to your students. Google Classroom does make it easier for you to create a whole lesson plan on it. You can build up an assignment with a description as well as with videos, links, and more than one document at a time. This helps to put all of the lessons in one place.
- Make your announcements: if you are worried about your students not being able to find the information that they need, you can place all of the announcements into your Google Classroom. You can communicate with your students, leave comments, set up assignments and announcements and more.
- Save on paper; you no longer need to spend so much time worrying about copying pages or making sure that you have extra copies when students lose the assignment It can all be done in one place, saving you some time and a

lot of paperwork in the process.

- Make turning in assignments easier: as a teacher you may have come to dread the process of turning in assignments. Some students will make excuses for losing the paper or forgetting about a due date. Some will ask for various copies of the homework assignment. And others just left it at home so it is all going to be late. This can be such a hassle for the teacher to deal with overall. But with the help of Google Classroom, you will be able to put the assignment with all of the instructions online, the due date will be automatically updated to Google Calendar, and your students can even turn it in online to save some time.
- Reduce cheating: since all of the documents for the class are not going to be placed into a shared file, there isn't the temptation for students to look through other answers and cheat on their homework.
- Collaboration: the teacher is able to share documents and then choose if the students re able to view that documents or even make changes to it. Creating a new document and then allowing all of the students in that class to be able to access and edit to it is a great way to set up a group project that everyone is able to work with together.
- Start a new discussion: starting discussions is a great tool to use inside of Google Classroom. It allows you to hear a bit from everyone, even the students who may not be the best at speaking up when they are in class. You can post a few discussion questions and then ask all of the students to comment and reply a few times for their grade.
- Email the feedback: when you return some of the assignments to the students, you can provide a note that is known as a global note, to all of the students if you notice that there is a common mistake that everyone is making that you would like to fix. Or you can send feedback to individual students if you want to discuss the

grade or the assignment with them. Google Classroom offers you the ability to post a note or a comment right to the assignment and the student is even able to comment back if they have a concern or a question. This makes the learning a bit more interactive for everyone involved.
- Create new folders: this used to be something that was kind of a cumbersome process through Google Drive, but it is now a process that is going to be done automatically. The teacher will have a folder that helps hold onto each assignment, which makes it easier for all of the students involved.
- Email students. You no longer will need to create a group of email addresses because you will be able to pick out the option to email everyone at once if you would like.
- Find out which students need more help. Google Classroom is a great tool because it is going to let you know the status of assignments from each student. You will be able to go through and see which students have not finished an assignment and then decide from there if you need to provide them with some extra help or not. You can even send out an email notification to these students who seem to be falling behind, offering some tips or some other help so that they can get the assignment done.
- Using the Calendar: this is one of the best features that you are going to enjoy from Google Classroom. You will find that it is really helpful to be able to assign a new assignment and the information is automatically placed on Google Calendar. Students will be able to look at this calendar and see what they have to finish and by when. There are no more excuses for later work or a million questions about when a due date is because Google Classroom will take care of it all for you.

There are so many great features that students and teachers are going to be able to enjoy when it comes to working in Google

Classroom. Teachers and students alike are going to be able to get some great results when they choose to use Google Classroom for their needs because it enhances communication, learning, and so much more!

Conclusion

Thank for making it through to the end of *Google Classroom: Teacher Guide to Google Classroom.* Let's hope it was informative and able to provide you with all of the tools you need to achieve your goals of

The next step is to get set up with working on Google Classroom. You will need to set it up so that you can either join the domain that your administer has set up, or you can set up your own domain and get started that way. Once the application has been processed and you are ale to get the Google Education App, you will then be able to set up your very own class in nontime.

Once you are all on the Google Classroom, you are able to set up as many classes as you need, invite students to come join the classes, send out assignments and announcements, add in more teachers, and so much more. There are so many things that you are able to do in order to make your teaching experience so much better.

When you are ready to find a way to personalize your learning environment, keep students on the same page, and to ensure that you are getting the results that you are looking for, make sure to check out this guidebook and learn everything that you need to make Google Classroom work for you.

Finally, if you found this book useful in any way, a review on Amazon is always appreciated!

Made in United States
Orlando, FL
24 June 2024